WHITE EAGLE'S
LITTLE BOOK
OF COMFORT
FOR THE
BEREAVED

*There is an audio CD of
much of this book, entitled*
COMFORT FOR THE BEREAVED,
*and a much fuller book from which some of the
passages in this book are taken, entitled*
A GUIDE TO LIVING WITH DEATH AND DYING

*Some further books of sayings and
short readings by White Eagle*
THE BOOK OF STAR LIGHT
PRAYER, MINDFULNESS AND INNER CHANGE
THE SOURCE OF ALL OUR STRENGTH
THE STILL VOICE
TREASURES OF THE MASTER WITHIN
WHITE EAGLE'S LITTLE BOOK OF
HEALING COMFORT

*For a full list of White Eagle publications,
including the annual Calendar of
White Eagle's sayings, go to
www.whiteagle.org
or send for a catalogue to one of
the addresses given at the end of this book*

WHITE EAGLE'S
Little Book
of Comfort for
the Bereaved

WHITE EAGLE LODGE PUBLISHING
NEW LANDS : LISS : HAMPSHIRE : ENGLAND

First published June 2007
© The White Eagle Publishing Trust, 2007
Reprinted 2015
Reset and reprinted 2020

British Library
Cataloguing-in-Publication Data
A catalogue record for this book is available
from the British Library

ISBN 978-0-85487-240-4

Set in Monotype Calisto at the Publisher and
printed and bound in the UK
by Halstan Printing Group, Amersham

Contents

Preface

This book and a matching CD represent the third compilation of White Eagle's teaching on the subject of dying, bereavement, and continuing life. The readings in the main are a distillation of teaching in the much fuller book, A GUIDE TO LIVING WITH DEATH AND DYING, although they also include new material. The CD, entitled COMFORT FOR THE BEREAVED, is a slightly-shortened audio recording of the passages, read by contemporary readers, and is available separately from the White Eagle Lodge (www.whiteagle.org).

INTRODUCTION

Death—our own or that of a loved one—is possibly the thing that we all fear the most. From the moment of birth the one unavoidable fact for us all is that one day our body will die. One of the most helpful aspects of the White Eagle teaching is that it gives a very clear statement about death and how we survive it. It gives a reasonable, logical explanation for what happens when the physical body ceases to contain us, and also gives a convincing picture of the life beyond death. In addition, it encourages everyone to understand that it is possible to have a continuing relationship at the inner level with loved ones who have passed on. It is not necessary for there to be any sort of 'medium' involved, or anyone else, for this contact to be made.

The White Eagle teaching and path of unfoldment offer everyone, even those who do
not feel they have any particular psychic or
spiritual gift, the possibility of experiencing
very real proof of the continued presence of
their loved ones and establishing ongoing
communion with them.

One reason for this is that White Eagle
also offers a symbol or mantra to assist in
the communion we seek with the world of
spirit, with the Great Spirit, and with our
loved ones. It is a shining six-pointed star.

This unique and accessible book of teaching selects some of the most comforting,
helpful and informative passages of White
Eagle's teaching on death. It gives a way forward, through the grief and shock that death
almost inevitably generates. The readings
give an account of the life after death which
may provide genuine comfort both for the

bereaved and for those who fear death. In the book, White Eagle describes the very process of death and the role played by the angel of death. White Eagle guides us in ways of finding peace and comfort after a death and helps us to make a beautiful spiritual contact with loved ones in the world of light. What he describes is not theoretical, but is a real insight into the soul's experience of life after death. The book speaks to everyone, yet helps us to know that in our personal experience of death, we are never alone.

Chapter One

DEATH IS ALSO BIRTH

BELOVED children of earth, we know that in most hearts there is grave fear about what lies the other side of death, the side you do not see; and our desire in giving this message is to bring to you consolation and comfort. Most people know only the physical aspect of death. They watch a friend in what appears to be the agony of death, but which is far more often a quiet, peaceful passing away of the consciousness. That is all: a passing away of the consciousness from the physical body. But it leaves desolation in the heart of the onlooker, a great fear. It is to bring you consolation and perhaps a deeper understanding that we speak on this subject.

When death draws near, angels always gather in the home and at the bedside of the one about to depart. You may think of the angel of death as an angel of darkness and terror, but you are wrong. The angel of death is like the Holy Mother: all love and tenderness, gentleness and beauty. When a soul receives the call from earth to heaven, loving preparation is made in the spirit world for the reception of that soul. If only people could have their vision clear enough to see that welcome being made ready, they would never be sad at death. They would be as happy as when a child is born into life down here, indeed more happy.

Once there, the soul is laid gently on a soft couch facing what you would call open windows, or a space in the room open to the air.

The perfume of flowers from the garden of the home steals in. Those who love that dear one are waiting. As soon as its consciousness awakens, the new arrival is greeted by someone beloved and familiar. Remember that there is always someone who loves them waiting in the spirit world for those who pass on. No-one journeys from the earth to the world of spirit without meeting with a loving welcome, because every living soul has some loved one in the world of spirit.

What of the dear ones left behind to mourn their loss? Angels are with them also, and bring to their earthly friends a spiritual food that can sustain and give them strength. It is the materiality and shadow of the earth mind that causes pain and grief. You can prove this for yourselves when you tune in to the realms of light, when all burdens will slip away. When you are functioning in full consciousness in that higher world, you will have no burdens. You will know happiness, for you are in a state of happiness. And so, my children, you will learn from this that happiness—heaven—is within the soul.

What we say will, we hope, help you understand that there is no separation at death. By this we mean that when a soul passes on to the next state, which is usually the astral world, it finds itself in exactly the same state of life as the one it goes to every night. When you are what is called 'asleep', you are living for a time in the astral world, and there you are meeting former companions of your earthly life. It is all a matter of harmony; and you are drawn to those with whom you are in harmony. So for the one who passes, there is not the separation you imagine, because in deep sleep all meet on that plane of reunion. Your sleeping here is like the waking over there on the astral plane. So you must dismiss all thought of separation when the change called death comes.

We repeat, there is no separation. There is no death. It is just a continuation of conscious life.

Chapter Two

FREEDOM

WHEN, as it does to everyone in due course, the time comes for you to lay aside your own physical body, or to see a loved one of yours withdraw from theirs, don't concentrate your thoughts on the physical body. It disintegrates and goes the way ordained for it by Mother Earth, by Mother Nature.

Just above the still form of the one who has passed on, you will see the gates opening. The veil of materialism of the earthly life will be drawn aside. You will see the spirit of your loved one freed to a world of heavenly beauty. You will see him or her overwhelmed with joy to meet loved ones who have long since passed away. Your joy will be in seeing what they have hoped for coming to them. You will see that they meet in a heavenly garden, in heavenly scenery and amid beauty indescribable in earthly language. And more than this: you will see upon their faces the heavenly happiness that fills their hearts when they find that there is no death.

In the spirit world, there is the most perfect plan for the reception of every soul who leaves a physical body. A messenger is sent to welcome the newly-released soul from the physical body, to welcome them into a world of peace and beauty, a spiritual beauty such as you cannot understand.

When you see, in the outer world, violence and what appears to be the most terrible suffering, brought about by the ignorance and the selfishness of human kind, do remember the mercy of God and the power of God! The soul that is apparently leaving a tortured body is mercifully cloaked by a divine power. Inside, it is filled with indescribable joy and surprise: 'Oh, this is wonderful, this is beautiful, where am I?'. And the friend by his or her side will answer: 'You are with friends; we have so much of interest to show you'. Then that soul is led away to objects that are familiar, but beautiful. So you see, from our side of life death is non-existent: all is living eternally in that divine Love, that divine Intelligence.

Make no mistake about it, every soul who comes over to our life is befriended. It does not matter who he or she is, or what harm the soul has done; or how wrong it may have been according to earthly standards. That soul is welcomed by a friend, one who really gives love. Many come back to those on earth with the same message: 'It is so beautiful over here. We have found peace'.

Will you come with us into the infinite and eternal garden and walk on the velvety turf, breathing into your tired etheric bodies the vibrations of health and power and buoyancy that are here? Be recharged, etherically, as you and we walk together on this green carpet!

Do you see the flowering shrubs, the blazing colours in this massed group of flowers? Do you hear the trickling water as it tumbles down the rocky cleft; and do you see the nature spirits splashing and laughing in the glorious crystal water? Life abounds: on all the blooms, on the bushes and in the trees, the little fairies are at work. You may hear the birds singing in praise and thanksgiving for their life. And you, the human being, the greatest of all God's creatures, are caught up in this grand brotherhood of life. We become aware, as we walk over those lands, of happy groups of friends (the companions of our spirit, our loved ones in the world of light). We are in the company of a grand brotherhood; harmony, peace and goodwill reign supreme.

Chapter Three

TRUST

YOU WILL be sustained. Whatever happens to you physically, you can be certain that underneath are the everlasting arms. But we have more to tell you than that; we tell you that there is a plan for your spiritual development, and all that happens is a step forward on that path. Try to cultivate confidence in God. God is merciful, and when you have to endure sickness, or anticipate an ordeal, have no fear. Fear is your greatest enemy.

Learn to conquer fear, and to trust the love of your heavenly Father and Mother.

Cast out fear, and you will be at peace. And so we ask you to resign all your fears, all your problems, to your heavenly Father–Mother God: to that great triangle of wisdom, love and power.

Maybe you are very sad at times, my child, but you must try to relinquish the anguish and the anxieties which you are inclined to re-live. Try to steady that emotional body. When you feel so overcome, stand erect with your spine straight and heels together and breathe in the breath of life. Try to feel that light and power coming right through your body, strengthening you, giving you poise of spirit. For great love enfolds you....

God bless you. God *is* blessing you.

God knows the suffering of His–Her creatures.... God knows, God loves, God is merciful. Remember above all that God is merciful, which means that out of pain and suffering and sorrow will come a beautiful unfoldment as a flower in bud gradually unfolds in the warmth and the light of the sun. Each one of you is like that flower, gradually unfolding. We can never take your experience away from you, only help you to carry your burden, by loving you and bringing about demonstrations in your life of the loving care of God.

So may you look forward with hope, not only to the time ahead of you now, but to all the years ahead. When another time comes (the period of rest or passivity, when you enter the world beyond) may you realize that it will be like passing from a darkened room into a sun bath!

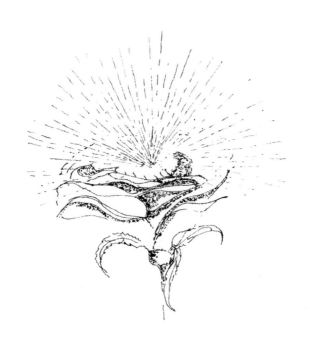

Chapter Four

THANKFULNESS

PERHAPS a loved one has passed away? All the bereaved has left to him or her is a corpse—nothing more. You know, my friends, the agony this brings? But is it true separation? Only for those living in the mortal mind, in the material self. The arisen soul has gone forward into the light—to a state the mourner, the one who is left behind, can also reach if he or she would rise above the limitations of personal grief.

We should like to say one thing in particular to those of you who are bereaved. It is that in every case release has been the most beautiful experience for each of those individuals. It has been as easy as sleeping and awakening into the eternal and infinite garden and to life in the spirit world. Be thankful: it is time for thankfulness. Be thankful for the love and the life that you have enjoyed with them. More than this, be thankful for their release into a world of indescribable beauty and peace, happiness and fresh opportunity. Never forget that all around you are these radiant ones, the brothers and sisters of the light, and your own loved ones, who are so close to you in spirit. And you will say: 'Why can't I see them if they are so close?'. You *can* see them. And if the time hasn't arrived yet when you see them, nevertheless you *will* do so.

More than this, you may feel the gentle presence of your loved one. It may be like a beautiful breeze. You may feel the gentle touch on face or hand or arm, and you may brush it aside and say: 'It is my imagination'. Do not be too sure. Keep your balance, certainly. Be wise and balanced, but be receptive to the heavenly breeze, the heavenly light, the white garment, the gentle touch, the sweet music of the heavens.

You will hear their voice. You will hear in your heart what they wish to say to you. Be happy that they are alive and free and can meet you clearly in that heavenly garden.

Relax, be still. There is nothing to fear. Let yourself float in the ocean of the Infinite Love. Be still and know God.

Just rest; feel that you are sustained on a great ocean of strength and of unending peace. Your needs are all known to the hosts of invisible and angelic presences and every true need will be supplied. Have confidence in the Source of your life. Be still. All is well.

Chapter Five

DEVELOPING IMAGINATION

IMAGINATION, which is so little under-
stood, is the doorway into our world—into
the higher ethers, the higher and finer etheric world. The key that unlocks the door is
hanging in your heart. It is unlocked through
love, love of God, love of all that is good.
Truth, wisdom, light, beauty are the keys
that unlock the door of imagination, which
takes you into that world of spirit.

We are not limited and bound as you are
by the flesh, and we come back to tell you
that there is no death, and that your loved
ones are very close beside you. Those who

can open the door of their imagination will see them. They come to reassure you, to love you and help you to traverse the path of life which will lead you, without fail, into a life of infinite beauty, here, while you are enclosed in a body.

Remember to walk your way through life in the full consciousness that in body and spirit you and we are all one. All people are one. You cannot injure any of God's creatures without injuring yourself. You cannot love and give kindness to any of God's children without receiving love and kindness yourself. This is the message of what we call the *at-one-ment*.

You must cultivate imagination, not only imagination of places and form, but imagination of feeling. This is what is wrong with humanity at its present stage of evolution. It has no imagination of the effect of its own speech and emotions upon other creatures, including other people. Imagination is the primary quality for you to develop, because it is only through imagination that you learn the feelings of others. And this, my dear ones, is the key to love.

When you have developed your power of imagination so that you can put yourself in the place of other human beings, you can put yourself in the place of all nature, into the place of the animal kingdom, and be sensitive to the suffering that can be inflicted on animals by people. When you have developed your power of imagination, when you have developed your sensitivity and your feeling, and when you can feel through your imagination the suffering and pain of other people, then you are developing that true love, the power of love.

Someone asked us once what our world is

like. We will give you a picture of the spirit world, for there is so much confusion when you are told that the world we come from is a mental world. It is true that it is a mental world insofar as it is composed of thought. Let us explain it to you in this way, that when you develop your power of imagination and the power of love which all these other things promote and stimulate, you will find that in your meditations you will see beautiful things, and not ugly things. You will see the world of God. That world is governed by love.

The more you develop this sensitivity to the needs and the feelings of your companions, the more you are developing your vision and your hearing and your appreciation of beauty. You are developing your soul-qualities. So when you no longer have a physical body, when you just get up and leave it lying down there, you will have no more interest in it, and you will find yourself in a spirit state of life.

You cannot resuscitate that physical body. But you want a body of some kind. You want senses to enable you to move around and see where you are. Unless you have developed those senses in your earth life by being kind and loving, by appreciating the glory of nature, the beauty of flowers and trees, the joy of the song of birds, the glory of the sunrise and the sunset; unless you have developed an appreciation of God's gifts in your own being—that is, the gift of hearing sound, beautiful sounds, and of seeing beautiful things in the earth plane—you will be quite a long time in the spirit world before you can actually see and feel its glory. But one day at last you will be able to say: 'Oh, I am happy! God is everywhere around me. I know the meaning of joy. I know the meaning of happiness, and I am free'.

There can be no death, only creation and dissolution, coming together again in creation—and so on throughout the rhythm of life. When you have reached to the centre of truth—which is God, is spirit—you will be only conscious of eternally living, and will not be separated at any time from those you love. Some people will call that level of consciousness that you can touch, cosmic consciousness.

If you who are reading our words have lost dear ones by the falling away of the physical body, the release of the spirit—if you have lost the physical form—then we advise you to use your thought-power and see your loved ones. Think of them, speak to them, spirit to spirit. This takes a little time for you to understand, but if you persevere in your quiet moments thinking of the spirit world as a world of eternity—always there, always being brought into the vision, into manifestation—you will eventually live in that consciousness of life. You will be aware of life not in all its drabness and suffering and restriction in a physical body, but aware of a life that is free like a lark in the sky.

Chapter Six

LOOKING WITHIN

W HEN a soul leaves the physical body, it is in reality passing inward to an inner state of being. Think of the physical life as an outward life, in which you are immersed in matter of a coarse condition. Away from your body, your world will be of a finer and more malleable matter, matter more easily responsive to thought and emotion.

The ordinary souls of ordinary people— the dear humanity we love for their kindliness—after death again meet their friends, not only of the incarnation they have just finished, but sometimes companions of former incarnations. When you come to the spirit world, all the beauty, the love, the selflessness and devotion which you have poured out on others is manifest in your home and in your surroundings. Many souls, when awakening on the astral plane, say: 'All I can see is God—God in the flowers, God in the trees, God in form, God in the landscape, God in everything! I am in God, and God is in me. We are inseparable'. And yet the person retains his or her individuality. The more Godlike he or she is, the more beautiful his surroundings, her appearance. In every way he or she is a channel for God.

It is really a plane of reunion where the soul enjoys an enhanced life, continuing the many different interests such as music, painting, literature and perhaps science, which it enjoyed when on earth. The soul enjoys new freedom and the opportunity of learning more of the particular subject which attracts it. Intense joy can come to the musician as he or she experiences the joys of music without limitation, and the same applies to art. For instance, you may love music and yet be unable to express yourself through music in your present life. On the astral plane, that desire will be granted if you wish. You will find that you are able to play the instrument of your choice without limitation. If you longed to be part of an orchestra or choir, you would find yourself a member, on equal terms with anyone else there. Perhaps you long to paint; you long to create beauty—and you will be able to do so. On the astral plane, all limitations fall away and the soul perfectly expresses itself in colour, form or music. This brings intense happiness.

Every soul discovers in the course of

its journey that God is no harsh judge but merciful and loving. The soul has only to turn towards God to receive all the help it needs, even as a child runs to its parents for comfort and love. Every soul receives its due in the afterlife, and what it receives is administered with mercy and love. Usually, when the soul has passed through a period of bliss and quietude, absorbing the truth that it needs to enable it to grow, it will again start its downward journey into incarnation.

Chapter Seven

THE BANISHMENT OF FEAR

AT THE beginning of our mission on the earth plane, we were given a charge. We were told that our work on that plane was to help remove from the minds of men and women the mad fear of death. And this is the purpose of our mission: to help you all to banish all fear of death you might have. Now, you are fearful of the unknown, not only of the unknown in the world of spirit, but also your own future. You are fearful of all that you do not know and all that you do not understand. We come only to open little shutters in your mind, give you a little glimpse here and there of the truth of spirit life, the truth about the journey upon which you are set.

We should like you to picture this: in the spirit (you know from your Bible) there are *many mansions.* Shall we say, there are many centres of service? There is an infinity of helpers who are sent out by their master to help. You would be surprised if you could see the way the spirit world is organized for the help of souls—whether souls on the physical plane or souls on the plane immediately beyond the physical life, souls who may be in a state of darkness. Every one of these souls is known. Do you remember Jesus saying that *not a sparrow falls to the ground without your Father?* And that *the very hairs of your head are all numbered?* And so it is. From these centres of service there is sent forth a group, or groups, of ordinary men and women. According to the needs of the soul who is in a place of darkness, so the helper is chosen, the right kind of helper, the helper who can most easily or readily get into communication with the soul who is being helped.

When it happens that those people who have no knowledge of the spirit life are suddenly flung out of physical life, we want you to know that they are instantly taken care of. When they walk out of their body they do not know what has happened to them. But they walk out and find someone, a friend, waiting for them.

Think of this, and if you have at any time had cause to be doubtful or anxious about anyone you love—anyone who has, either through war or accident, been flung into the spirit world—and you wonder what happened to them, then never forget these faithful servers, who move together in groups, carrying the light, going into the dark places.

Many times people on earth who are bereaved will have received messages from spirit saying 'I was caught up in a light' or 'I saw a light, a blessed light in the darkness, and it moved and I followed it'. As they followed that light, they would have very soon found friends, kindly friends waiting to give them exactly what they most needed at that time. We want you to understand that the world of spirit is very natural, very normal in all the things which the lower etheric manifestation of a person still wants (because for a while he or she still retains desires of the flesh) and a comforting meal might be heaven to some soul who has just left the physical body. All these things, good things, are prepared for him or her. *Death is a very beautiful experience.* The masses concentrate on the sordid aspects, but to the soul pressing forward, death is glorious.

Chapter Eight

FOLLOW THE LITTLE LIGHT

YOU LONG to have physical contact with your loved ones who have passed onwards. We cannot blame you, for we understand that longing to touch the hand of the one that has gone and to see the vacant chair filled. 'We long to feel their touch', you will say. Yes, we know; we know that longing—but there is an even better way than holding on to the physical body. Remember, a physical body is merely a form of dress, which is something you will fully appreciate when you come to shed your own present one. On earth, you feel rather pleased to have some fresh clothes. When your old ones are tired, you send them away. But when it comes to the physical clothing, however old and decrepit it is, you still long to keep it with you.

Now this is a bridge you have to cross. We do not mean the bridge from our world to your world that we have been speaking about. We do not mean the bridge you cross at death. We mean a bridge that you cross in full consciousness while you are on earth.

What do we mean by this? We mean that while you are living in a physical body and in a very material world, you have to strive to realize that you are not your body, but that you are a spirit being, clothed for a time in a certain body. When you can look beyond that clothing and that material life, you will see a much finer world, a world that is quite as real and solid as the physical matter, but one composed of much finer and more sensitive matter.

One way truly to become aware that you are not your body is through constant endeavour to accept that there are other worlds in which you, the son–daughter of God, can live. You are bound by the intellect and your body, but when you turn to the deep holy sanctuary which is within your soul, then you receive a manifestation, a demonstration. It comes not through a physical body, but through a spiritual power that is far more convincing than a physical body. And why? Because in that holy sanctuary a jewel resides: Christ, the Son of God your Creator.

When you contact that spirit power you are convinced—you *know*—that you are an eternal being, and that all of the human race are eternal beings too. You know that there is a state of life beyond the present house of flesh—a world of beauty, of ever-unfolding glory and opportunity. There, those souls who have shed their old form of dress, and have let go their contact and longing for physical matter, find themselves in a world of beauty and harmony and brotherhood of the spirit. They find that they have companions who understand their innermost needs. They find that these companions will guide them to the exact place where they will find happiness. Not in singing psalms all day, not in lying about doing nothing, but in being engaged in some study or pursuit which is after their own heart: that is where their happiness lies.

As for those who have left the earth through being sacrificed in a war—something that has come about through the ignorance of the world—we can tell you that they find a particular comfort and happiness in our world. Sacrifice of the individual, self-sacrifice, brings great blessing to the soul. It wipes away so much of what you would call 'sin'. No-one 'innocently suffers', because the so-called innocent sufferers are gathered into the great arms of love. These conditions of war that come to the earth plane, although they are brought about by ignorance and stupidity, are turned to good effect. No-one is sacrificed in vain, and with war there comes a corresponding push forward in the evolution of humanity. All the time spiritual growth continues in you, and not only spiritual growth but mental growth. Better conditions of life are the result of past suffering.

There is a little light inside you, a voice, an urge. Follow it, follow it, dear ones, and it will lead you to a place of great beauty where your view is expanded. In this place you can really enjoy the blessing of that undoubted love of the great Master who has, within his heart, you and all your loved ones. It is for you in yourself, by your thoughts, by your aspirations, to reach that level on the mountain where you know there is no separation in life.

It is so simple: the key is so simple—and as the ancients said, the key hangs in your heart. If you wish to unlock the door of paradise, of happiness, of beauty in the world of spirit, the key lies within you. It is simply love. Love one another, love life, love your Creator. And know within you that the one you love is as close to you now as ever: closer than ever. The one you love comes to you so clearly. You do not see the physical body, but it may be you can in your memory hear that physical voice, and you know in your heart what that voice is saying to you.

Chapter Nine

THE STRENGTH OF LOVE

CAN YOU analyze what you feel for the ones you love? No, you do not know why or how you love, but you know that the consciousness of love brings to your soul beauty, light and encouragement and peace. Treasure love; do not take it lightly, or for granted. It is something which raises you heavenwards, and without love your life would be darkened. Think of yourself as being held within that light which is the heart of all creation, which manifests as love.

Your nearest and dearest bring to you comfort, comfort for your body and for your mind. If some separation takes place, there comes a loss of this comfort and earthly companionship; but if through understanding what death means you have reached beyond the earthly to the spiritual companionship, to an affinity of spirit, you have touched the wider, fuller love—a love which, although shown to you through the individual, is nevertheless not confined to that individual.

We come to you to help you to expand your consciousness to that world of light, which is interpenetrating your physical world. It is a great mistake to separate the levels of life by saying, 'we are down here on the earth', and 'the spirit world or heaven is up there'. We want you all to grow in the consciousness of this interpenetration of the higher worlds. We say 'higher worlds' not because they are set apart from you, but yet they are light worlds: they are not to be found in the dense material consciousness. They are instantly to be found when you open yourself in love. Your thoughts of love never fail to reach those you love who have passed onward. If you truly love your companion he or she is with you, closer than breathing, because both of you are part of God. You can never be separated from those you love, so long as you love them, and you love God; you are all one.

When you shed your body, oh, you are so light and young! It is a wonderful experience. Never grieve for the dead, and do not grieve for the living. They are all learning, all are learning. The unenlightened will say, 'I cannot understand a love that will cause suffering, will permit suffering, will allow itself to be withheld while witnessing suffering. Yet, only true love can thus see a loved one suffer; for then it knows that out of suffering comes goodness and truth and all the riches of heaven. Love must stand aside and watch suffering with a vision so clear that it knows that suffering is part of love's travail. Remember: if you love, dear ones, you will not try to prevent your loved one learning, but you will do all you can to help. This is wisdom: the mother-wisdom which foresees good born of suffering. You need have no fear for yourself, no fear of any living thing, because God holds you in His–Her arms.

Do not deny this. Do not say, 'No, I cannot believe it'. It is true, and you have to make yourself realize that it is true: that underneath, always, are the everlasting arms.

Chapter Ten

YOUR OWN RESURRECTION

CAN you comprehend freedom: freedom from all want and limitation, freedom from evil thoughts, freedom from pain? Can you imagine yourself free to give and share with all creatures and all human beings the wonderful life of God? The great initiate Jesus, the Christed one, has demonstrated to you that there is a life beyond the physical body, a life beyond death. You will remember the words written in your Bible, those that the woman spoke when she found the stone rolled away from the tomb: *They have taken away my Lord*. The stone is the mortal mind, the material mind, and that stone has to be removed. You are in your own tomb in a physical body, but the ministering angel comes to you and will remove the stone, enabling you to rise and come out of your physical body into a world of infinite beauty. The voice bewailed, *They have taken away my Lord, and I know not where they have laid him.* Now this is what you feel when you have lost a loved one. Where has she gone? Where is he now? Where has my darling child gone? But the Master returned and explained that he had not died. He had not been taken away, he was still there with them.

This is the most beautiful illustration of what you call death, or the passing of the soul from one condition, from one state of life, to the next. It is to this next world that the soul goes for refreshment and rest, and absorption of those things of the spirit which maybe it had glimpsed while in the tomb, but could not reach because the mortal mind was blocking the way. You may see an inanimate form lying there, but the spirit is freed, is alive, is able to overcome all the limitations of time and space.

There is doubt in the mind, fear about the actual passing out of the tomb into that heavenly state of life. But we wish to reassure you that if you surrender yourselves in quietness, in trust to the Great Spirit, there is nothing to fear, but everything in which to rejoice. You can think of being a prisoner on earth and then having the prison gate flung open, and you get out into the wide, wide life.

We will tell you, as far as we are allowed, what happens when the transition takes place from the physical body. Your loved one may appear to have a little struggle, or may not appear to have any struggle at all, but if there is a little struggle for breath, it does not affect your loved ones.

They are released from the physical body, they are borne on angel wings, or in the arms of the angels who are waiting for them, and they are carried away to the spirit world, and there they may be taken to a beautiful blue lake. Sometimes it is called the blue country because the atmosphere, the air, seems to be like the sky: blue, so clear, so fresh.

When they awaken from their sleep, their angel guide is with them, and they are told that if they wish they may take a plunge into that blue lake. Indeed, they are told they will feel better if they go for a bathe. So almost invariably the urge is so great, they have a beautiful swim in that blue lake; and it means that they are cleansed and purified of all earthly entanglements and unpleasant things. They are freed, cleansed, purified.

Then they rest for a time on the green bank, which is dotted with flowers. They see God; they understand that they are looking into God's world—seeing the life, the real life.

The colours in the world of spirit are not dull like your colours. To us, your colours are very dull; but in the world of spirit, nature, the trees, the flowers, even the very air itself, pulsate with colour, intensified colour. Our colours are not aggressive, but most harmonious; and the colours that we see in the spirit world have their vibration of harmony so that the colours are also music, the grand orchestra of infinity. This is what your loved ones go to. This is what you yourself will eventually reach.

Chapter Eleven

THE COMFORTER

WE KNOW, dear brethren, we know perhaps even more than you think, just how sorrowful you can be when a loved one is taken from your side, either by death of the physical body, or by misunderstanding. We know how bitter thoughts can creep in when the human emotions are very stirred up, so that you can only feel the bitterness of your own disappointment and grief. Everything around you looks black, and all life seems to be fading away from you because you are cut off from the source of your spiritual comfort, from love. Love is God, and when you have no love in your heart because you are bitter through grief or disappointment or misunderstanding, you do not know which way to turn. Then life is black indeed.

When the disciples were feeling completely isolated after Jesus' death, they were told to go to Jerusalem. To go to Jerusalem means to rise to a higher state of consciousness. There they were to wait in an upper room for the coming of their Comforter. The Comforter will come if you will aspire in consciousness to the upper room, which means the higher level of life.

In your thoughts, rise to that upper room and wait patiently and humbly in communication (that is, in love) with God. Then will come the outpouring of the spirit, the Comforter, even the spirit of truth. When the spirit of truth comes into your soul and heart you are comforted. If you would get love, then give love, and you will be comforted.

If you take the time to attune yourself daily (even if only for five minutes in the morning on waking, or at night before going to sleep); if you send out your thoughts to the divine spirit of love, then the Comforter will surely enter your heart. The Comforter will enter the heart of every one of you. You will know the meaning of the word 'comforter', and you will know what the Comforter is. You will not get this from any other person; although your closest friend or relative, who may be in harmony with you, can help you to be receptive. Each must make their own effort, though, and will then know with that inner knowing that this beloved, divine comforter is waiting to come. The realization may come through a flash of illumination, a flash perhaps in the silence of your own heart. Then you will know the truth about

God and the great almighty spirit, which is the ruler over all life—ruling over all manifestations of life, both on earth and beyond the earth.

Those of you who have lost relatives and friends—be comforted; but more than this, we beg you to endeavour to understand. We ask you to know that there is within you the power and the means to get in touch with those who have passed away from the darkness of earth. Material thinking brings down the shutter before your vision, but spiritual quickening, through your worship and love, brings a power superior to anything you can yet understand.

Many have experienced the truth of this message of the living God, for it is when the soul is bereft of a loved one that it is raised above the conditions of mortal life. The soul on earth longs for contact with the one that has gone from the body. Because of this urgent need for a spiritual comforter, the man or woman is raised in consciousness above all earthly things and finds him or herself alone and in the stillness. Then a great love wells up in the human heart: a simple, human love. This is the magnet that attracts the great light of heaven, and the light in the soul of the one who is bereft bursts forth so that the mind and the brain are illuminated. The Comforter enters the heart.

Chapter Twelve

THE PATH OF LIGHT

WHEN one of your number passes on, he or she finds a great welcome in our world. All of you have many friends in what you call the afterlife. But do not think of the invisible life as a place or condition that you cannot reach or be aware of while on earth. We come to speak for those who have passed through the veil of so-called death; those who have vanished from your sight for a while, but who are with you now. All around you are shining ones, who are thought by so many to be dead and gone. But, my children, there is no death—only life. All is life, eternal life.

Use your imagination at this moment. How would you feel if you left your physical body but hardly realized that you had left it, and you found yourself very close to your loved ones, to your family and friends—and yet they would not take any notice of you? You speak to them, you touch them, but they take no notice. Remember this image, and remember that within you God has placed the key, the key to a wider and grander and more beautiful life. You are so engaged in this earth world with earthly things, with physical things, with material things, that you have no time, no energy, no will, to think of the world around you, a world which is infinitely more beautiful than anything you can see or touch or hear with your physical senses.

You cannot contact spiritual life with your physical senses. You can only contact spiritual life, the life beyond the grave, with your spiritual senses. The time has come for you to awaken to your spiritual potentialities, to listen with your inner hearing, to use the senses of your celestial body. You are building and developing that spiritual body and the spiritual senses, which are replicas of the earthly senses, with the addition of a sixth sense, which some people call the intuition. This intuition is the inner sense of the spirit within, and the time has come when this inner sense is being developed.

The path before everyone is a path of light. The Son of God is the light. And God has put into the heart of every man, woman and child a light to guide them on that path which leads to the golden world of reunion and joy. You don't need to die physically to follow that path. All people will learn in time that they can reach that world of light by their own efforts—not when they leave the shell of the physical body, not when they change their garments, but at all times. Whatever they are doing, in the workshop, in the garden, in the business world, and wherever they are, people can think not only of matter, physical matter, but know also that they are for ever eternally linked, eternally united, with that divine spirit. They are always linked to the Father–Mother from whom they have come. That cord, that cord of light is ever there. Whatever you are doing on earth, just a thought and you are with your heavenly company. They have their own work to do, but their spirit is with you if you think about them. Mentally and quietly think of them, give your love and ask for their help, and be at peace within.

There are those seeking for conviction, because the hunger of love within urges them to find out where some loved one goes at death. One can obtain proof of the continuity of life after death. Never mind if the seeker only contacts the immediate next world, the lower astral plane. All serves a purpose, and is true; and it is right that communication and proofs should be given to the enquirer. But the deeper students of the mystery schools know that life is continuous. If you *know*, then the light is born within; you leave behind the search for evidence, which is but an endless repetition—like a gramophone record ever repeating the same thing. The light within says: 'I know; there is no death; my loved one cannot die: she, he, still lives'.

Chapter Thirteen

SEEING YOUR LOVED ONE

WHEN you have lost a loved one, may we remind you to recognize that it is only the physical body, like an outworn coat that has lost its usefulness, that you are missing. Hold fast to the truth that spirit is eternal, and that the personality, the beloved personality, is always there. Life changes, the scenes of life change; but the basic, the essential life of a person, the nature of the individual, is eternal. You have also been given the qualities within yourself, and the power, the gifts of the psyche, which enable you to make contact with spirit at will, and with the spirit of your loved ones.

You have only to think of your loved one to bring him or her close. Not careworn, not suffering; don't think of the pain and the distortion of the countenance during years of suffering. Think of your loved one with a face—a face like a shining Master, like Jesus or like Buddha, or any one of the great teachers. Think of him or her in that world of light. And remember that when you are there in meditation, or maybe in a dream, you will notice how happy they look. How smooth and beautiful then is the face of your loved one, showing quite clearly the feelings that are peaceful, joyous and thankful!

They bless you, they love you, and they want you to know that life for them has not ceased, but that they continue to live in a happier and freer condition. If you could only be there in the garden of reunion and remembrance you would know that there is no death. The separation is one that you, with your material minds, create. Your dear one is close beside you now. What you think habitually you become. If you habitually think along the lines of goodwill, of good thought, God thought, you draw nearer every day to your companions who dwell in the light.

These dear ones who are with you are also living in that state of harmony you call heaven, because they have heard the voice of goodness, of God. We wish you could see the happiness with which these people work in their own particular section in the spirit world. Each one is drawn, as by a magnet, to the very sphere and to the particular work that their soul most enjoys. Whatever the interest of your loved one, that interest is given to them in their life in spirit. Your loved ones are happy, and they rejoice in their service.

They come close to you and they whisper in your heart. Or, if you are trained in meditation and are able to release yourself from the burden and darkness of the earthly mind—so that you are able to enter the garden of remembrance in the spirit world—then your loved ones immediately come to you. It is the spiritual law of attraction. They come to you if you can imagine with your higher vision that you are with them. It is these inner powers and qualities of the spirit that you have to develop—so that you are always aware, conscious, of the companionship of your beloved ones; because in spirit there is no separation.

Chapter Fourteen

FROM OUR SIDE OF LIFE

BELOVED, we come to bring you the power of the spirit. So long as you live only in the consciousness of the physical life around you, it is as if you are living in a closed box; your vision is clouded, and you are looking as through a dark glass. Because of this, many of you grow weary and you need help and reassurance. You long to be raised beyond the limitations of the earth, to get a clearer vision of the life of the spirit which is all around you and which is your true home, the spirit life from which you have come to dwell in the flesh.

We are permitted to come to you from the world of spirit to bring you that power which will lift you up and give you peace of mind and strength of body.

We know someone on our side of life who used to be terrified of the possibility that one day she would lose her beloved family and be alone. Well, she never has been. She never will be. We gave her an experience which she has never forgotten. She found herself in the eternal world, with all her family about her, and she knew beyond a shadow of doubt that she could never be separated from those she loved.

No more can you. So long as you love them, and you love God, you are all one. If your aspirations during your physical life have been towards God, if you have served and loved all creatures, you will find yourself in a world of beauty with your own familiar things around you, and those you have loved on earth to greet you.

Every one of you here has, at some time, been through an ordeal, something you dreaded—perhaps an operation, perhaps giving birth to a child, or even the separation from a loved one. And although you have anticipated the worst, yet when the time came, a very gentle, sweet power came to you, and you were able to go through the feared ordeal with calmness, with a certain inner sweetness and love. So it is with death. Although the body may have to be discarded, the soul body is healed, and when it awakens after death, it is so well, so happy. However you pass away from your physical body, whether suddenly, by accident, or by a slow process of withdrawal, we would like you to understand that death is no dark vale, but rather it is a beautiful experience for the soul. Try to realize that you are not the physical body, any more than you are the clothes you wear. Your body is like the clothes you wear, and when the great transition comes to you, you will lay it aside as you lay aside your material clothing. But your true self, your invisible self, lies deep within you.

Indeed, what you call death is more truly an initiation of either lesser or greater degree for the human soul: and the culmination comes when the outer garment is committed to the fire. Then a great light breaks upon the soul. O children of earth, we beg you not to regard the passing of the soul from the body into immortal life as something to be dreaded! At the right time—for that time comes according to the law of God—the soul goes forth, not to lose its identity but to gain greater consciousness of God and awareness of the eternal light. Remember also when your friend is taken from you that the inner soul of man and woman knows the day and the time, the hour, when it has to leave this physical body. This may be an unconscious or a conscious knowledge, but the hour of passing cannot be altered by humanity, only by the Law of God. You must accept the loving wisdom of God and send the soul forth joyously, with your love and blessing, into that larger, happier, freer life. You must do this.

Lastly, remember that love disperses all mists. At the moment you may seem to be divided from those you love who have passed into the world of spirit. But you are not truly separated, although before you hangs a mist—sometimes a heavy fog. This fog is an individual's own creation. When he or she has light and love in the heart it warms and so shines through and disperses the mist.

Then that man or woman sees clearly into the worlds of higher ethers. There she sees her loved ones; he sees life as a whole. It is not a question of human kind being 'here' and the spirit 'over there' with a closed door between the two. Understanding reveals that life is universal, that the life of the spirit is identical with life on earth. True, the spirit world is a world more beautiful than this, but then it is made beautiful by the love which a soul learns to operate once it is away from the limitations with which it binds itself in the flesh.

Beloved, have you lost ones dear to you? Think of them, then, as in the sunlight of the worlds beyond, absorbing the very essence of the spirit. There is no death: progress ... progress ... growth ... a life-force ever moving onward, forward into the Sun.

This, my dear one (I speak to every indi-

vidual heart) this is our message! Hope …
hope … hope! Humanity makes progress; it
does not retrogress, and every method used
to bring about this birth into the spiritual life
is necessary. Look out upon the world that
is with tolerance and love and hope … the
best is yet to come.

Chapter Fifteen

THE ANGEL OF DEATH

DEAR ones, never fear anything. Never fear any ordeal. Never anticipate ills that you think are coming. Have no fear. Cast out fear and you will find peace.

Now we refer above all to the fear engendered in the mind by the words, 'through the dark vale of death'. Death is not a dark vale. Death is the most beautiful passage opening into a world of beauty. You people on earth fear death very much. Yet in reality it is not you who fear death. It is really only the body that fears it. Death is the angel sent to draw the unwilling bolt and set the spirit free. When the body dies, the angels of death, who are God's messengers, take the sleeping soul and bear it tenderly through the mists surrounding the earth, and place it on a couch in its new home. All earthly fear is left behind.

The wise know that there is no death. The wise grieve neither for the living nor for those who have passed into the spirit world. Yet you may know perfectly well that you will live on, that there is no death, and still there remains a niggling doubt in your mind, a little fear, about the actual passing out of the tomb of earth into that heavenly state of life. We are being true to you, my dear ones, when we tell you that if you surrender yourselves in quiet trust to the Great White Spirit (to the heavenly Father or to the divine Mother), you have nothing to fear, but everything in which to rejoice.

The moment comes when the man or woman has to 'die', as you call it. But of course the individual never dies. The spirit and the soul which clothes it is gently withdrawn and passes upward through the head. The physical body is left like an empty shell. In the heavenly state angels are waiting to receive the newborn soul.

The angel of death is present at every passing, no matter how it happens. That soul is caught up by the angel and is gently borne into the spirit. Usually that soul is in the form of a babe. The passing from the physical state to the next state is exactly the same as birth into this physical life; the soul appears to become like a little babe. The little form is built up above the physical body and is enfolded in the love of the angel of death. It is wrapped in the loving robe of the angel of death and borne away to its new state of life, where other angels wait to minister to it and gradually awaken it to a state of awareness of its new life.

*

You will not know when you take your last breath. You will be entirely unconscious that it is your last breath, but you will feel you are lighter. You are free. You will look around you, and you will see your familiar room, maybe your own bedroom, or wherever you are, a place that is familiar to you, and you will not know you have passed on.

It will gradually become a little misty, and you will think, 'this is a smoke screen!'. And that smoke will gradually dissolve, and you will find yourselves in a beautiful world of Light.

A Meditation

THE GARDEN OF REUNION

A S WE raise our consciousness, we see before us a pathway of light. As we follow the path of light we are drawn upwards, into the blazing six-pointed Star.

We are bathed in the pure, life-giving rays of the Christ Star. Peacefully we breathe in the light and feel it flowing through every cell of our being, releasing all the pain of the outer self. We are becoming still in the Star. Strong rays enfold us in wings of light as our guardian angel draws close to our inner most being.

We become stiller, more peaceful, as deep

in the heart a clear flame arises, grows and illumines our whole consciousness with a quality of God, divine peace, strength, courage, heavenly wisdom, joy, love. The angel's wings raise us heavenwards and we are bathed, immersed, irradiated with that God-quality which we need, deep within our soul.

*

And now, let us become aware of the beautiful garden of reunion. Each soul is taken to the quiet sanctuary to sleep until they are ready to awaken to the new life which awaits them. When they wake, they look out into a sunlit garden which is as dear and familiar to them as their most loved garden on earth; and thus they can walk into the sunlight to meet their beloved family and friends who are awaiting their coming. Stay a while here and commune with your loved ones....

THE WHITE EAGLE LODGE

www.whiteagle.org

The White Eagle Lodge is based on the profound yet gentle philosophy of White Eagle. Through his teaching we receive encouragement on a path of love, tolerance and service towards all life: a path which offers the development of inner peace and the awareness of our eternal, spiritual nature. There are many groups throughout the world, and they can be found by contacting the main centres given below. These centres offer services of healing, meditation, spiritual unfoldment and retreats.

White Eagle's teaching is presented in the printed and electronic books of the Lodge (www.whiteagle.org), alongside CDs and other publications; some are listed opposite the title page of this volume.

Readers wishing to know more of the work of the White Eagle Lodge should check the website above or contact The White Eagle Lodge, New Lands, Brewells Lane, Liss, Hampshire GU33 7HY.
In the Americas, please write to
The Church of the White Eagle Lodge
P. O. Box 930, Montgomery, Texas 77356
(tel. 936-597 5757; www.whiteaglelodge.org;
in Canada, use www.whiteagle.ca)
and in Australasia please write to
The White Eagle Lodge (Australasia)
P. O. Box 225, Maleny, Queensland 4552
(tel. 07-5494 4397; www.whiteaglelodge.org.au).
If using email, contact us via
enquiries@whiteagle.org (worldwide)
sjrc@whiteaglelodge.org (Americas)
enquiries@whiteeaglelodge.org.au (Australasia)